Words from the *Heart*

Words

from the

Heart

Card Greetings
for every
occasion

ARCTURUS

'Words without
thoughts never
to heaven go.'

From *Hamlet* by
William Shakespeare

ARCTURUS

This edition published in 2014 by Arcturus Publishing Limited
26/27 Bickels Yard, 151–153 Bermondsey Street,
London SE1 3HA

Thanks to Tim Glynne-Jones for editorial services

ISBN: 978-1-78212-778-9
AD003896UK

Printed in China

Contents

Introduction

'Letters have to pass two tests before they can be classed as good: they must express the personality both of the writer and of the recipient.'

E M Forster

The thought that counts

It's rare, these days, to receive anything pleasant in the mail. Bills, junk mail, free papers and flyers from local businesses make up most of it, the pile of waste paper causing a brief ripple of despondency before being transferred directly from doormat to recycling bin. So when you do receive something nice in your mailbox, the effect can be hugely uplifting. As Shakespeare put it in his play *Richard II*, 'Where words are scarce they are seldom spent in vain.' We could add to that, 'They are seldom received in vain either.'

The pen is no longer our chief tool when it comes to writing. These days, even children – or especially children – are more familiar with the computer keyboard or the mobile phone keypad than with putting pen to paper. And that's ok; it's all progress, provided we don't lose the skills we have developed over centuries. Words from the heart will hit their target whatever way you choose to send them, be it by email, text or post office. The important thing is that you send them, for their impact is always at least as great as the effort expended in writing them.

But there is still something particularly special, almost magical, about receiving a card or letter through the mail – all the more special these days for its scarcity. It is a more tangible, sensuous experience: holding the envelope, slicing it open, slipping the contents out, unfolding them and reading the words. We keep hold of cards and letters, sometimes for a lifetime; texts and emails are soon deleted. I think this is because there is an unspoken sentiment in the handwritten message: it says, 'I care enough to take the trouble to write this.' The recipient feels valued, loved and closer to the sender.

For there is effort involved. Finding paper and pen, thinking of the words, writing them neatly, addressing the envelope, buying a stamp and putting the letter in the post all require a degree of commitment that goes far beyond sending a text or email. But that's where the magic comes in; because all that effort becomes clearly evident to the person who receives your letter and the effect is to give them not just words, but feelings too – a virtual hug, if you like. In short, sincerity.

Sincerity is the key to all good writing and here the electronic forms fall short. Texts and emails can be notoriously ambiguous in their sentiments; ink on paper rarely is. Don't ask me why, that's just the way things seem to have evolved. So if you really want to send someone a message from the heart, I recommend you use a pen and give them the joy of receiving something uplifting through the mail.

How to use this book

I mentioned that sending a sincere handwritten message through the post takes some effort and the biggest effort of all is thinking of the words. Where do you start? Some messages are very difficult to get right. A condolence card, for example, treads a fine line between concern and being patronizing; a love letter must be flattering without being corny.

This book exists to get you started, to trigger your own words and ideas by offering examples that you can adapt to your specific scenario. There are words for all occasions and for all recipients. You can take my examples in their entirety if you feel they do justice to the sentiments you wish to express, or you can mix and match the messages, taking the parts that you like or you feel are particularly apt for your requirements, and putting together your own sincere and touching messages.

At the back of the book is a calendar for you to note down dates to remember so that you don't forget to write when the time comes. And there's space to jot down some notes, as you pick up ideas by reading through the book. Writing is a skill that improves with practice, so the more you write, the easier you will find it is to come up with the right form of words.

For further inspiration, I've included ten famous letters positioned at regular intervals throughout the book – letters penned by famous people down the ages. Each of these displays a level of sincerity and eloquence that will hopefully put you in the right frame of mind to master your own words from the heart.

Famous Letters

Sullivan Ballou

Ballou fought in the Union Army in the American Civil War and died in battle a week after writing these words.

July 14, 1861
Camp Clark, Washington

My very dear Sarah:
The indications are very strong that we shall move in a few days—perhaps tomorrow. Lest I should not be able to write again, I feel impelled to write a few lines that may fall under your eye when I shall be no more . . .

I have no misgivings about, or lack of confidence in the cause in which I am engaged, and my courage does not halt or falter. I know how strongly American Civilization now leans on the triumph of the Government and how great a debt we owe to those who went before us through the blood and sufferings of the Revolution. And I am willing to lay down all my joys in this life, to help maintain this Government, and to pay that debt . . .

Sarah my love for you is deathless, it seems to bind me with mighty cables that nothing but

Omnipotence could break; and yet my love of Country comes over me like a strong wind and bears me unresistibly on with all these chains to the battle field.

The memories of the blissful moments I have spent with you come creeping over me, and I feel most gratified to God and to you that I have enjoyed them for so long. And hard it is for me to give them up and burn to ashes the hopes of future years, when, God willing, we might still have lived and loved together, and seen our sons grown up to honorable manhood, around us. Something whispers to me—perhaps it is the wafted prayer of my little Edgar, that I shall return to my loved ones unharmed. If I do not my dear Sarah, never forget how much I love you, and when my last breath escapes me on the battle field, it will whisper your name. Forgive my many faults and the many pains I have caused you. How gladly would I wash out with my tears every little spot upon your happiness . . .

Birthdays

'Age is an issue
of mind over matter.
If you don't mind,
it doesn't matter.'

Mark Twain

FRIENDS

Wishing you a very happy birthday. Congratulations on another year of good deeds, kind words and warm feelings.

Like a fine wine, you just get better and better with age. Here's wishing you a perfectly balanced birthday with a delightfully robust finish.

Here's to you on your birthday. Another year older but your charm and humor remain as youthful as ever.

★ ★

When the world works right, good things happen to and for good people and you are definitely good people. Happy birthday!

Best wishes on your birthday.
I hope the next year will be another
vintage one in a *grand cru* life.

**Here's to another milestone on
an epic journey. With every step
you grow wiser and more far-
sighted. It's just the nearer stuff
that gets harder to focus on.**

★ ★

Wishing you a day
that is as special in
every way as you are.
Happy birthday.

It's your birthday, a time to pause and reflect on all that you have dreamed of and all that you have achieved. From where I'm standing, you have every reason to feel satisfied.

Once a year the world dances to your tune, sings your song and bangs your drum. It's your birthday. Enjoy the music.

I was going to tell you what a wonderful, generous, thoughtful, amusing, charming person you are, but then I thought it would only embarrass you. So I'll just say this instead. Happy birthday, gorgeous!

The world turns and with each
revolution you grow that
little bit more wonderful.
Warm-hearted wishes to a dear
friend on your birthday.

★ ★

*Wishing you health and
happiness on this special day.
May your birthday bring you
all the joy you give to others
throughout the rest of the year.*

*Many happy returns on your
birthday. Sadly we can't be
with you, but we are hugging
you in our hearts.*

Look, I remembered your birthday!
How could I forget someone
as memorable as you?
Happy birthday!

*Well, you are another year older
and you haven't changed a bit.
That's great because you are perfect
just the way you are. Happy
birthday!*

Celebrate your birthday today. Celebrate being happy every day.

★ ★

Don't be sad just because it's your
birthday. It could be worse – it could
be mine and I could be a whole year
older. Happy birthday!

Sincere best wishes on your birthday.
May the coming year bring you health,
happiness and adventures beyond your
wildest dreams.

Wishing you the birthday you deserve: magnificent, hilarious, spectacular and expensive!

★

Congratulations on your birthday. Enjoy the celebrations, cherish the memories and embrace the laughter. This is your day.

★

Wishing you joy and laughter
on your birthday.
May you spend the day basking in the
love we all feel towards you.

Happy birthday! I hope this day sees your dreams come true and your doubts proved false. You deserve all the happiness that comes your way.

Another year older, but your talents never wither.
Long may you continue to blossom.

★

You are a gift to the world. How's that for a reverse birthday wish? Happy birthday!

★ ★

**The world turns, the years go by, but your light, like the sun, remains constant.
Have a wonderful birthday, sunshine!**

When we're young we crave excitement, when we're old we crave contentment. May your birthday bring you all the excitement and contentment you desire.

★

I've been meaning to tell you all year how wonderful you are. Now I guess everyone's doing it. Happy birthday!

Congratulations on another year successfully negotiated. You're the business. Take a moment to pat yourself on the back before you roll your sleeves up for the next one.

FAMILY

I may not have told you often but I want you to know that you are the best Dad anyone could have and I'm really lucky to have you. Happy birthday!

Happy birthday, Grandma! Thank you for giving me your time and understanding and for showing me the value of selflessness.

★ ★

You gave me life and love and I will never forget that, but on your birthday we celebrate the fact that once the same was done for you. Have a lovely day, Mom!

Here's to you on your special day.
You put the grand
in Grandpa!

★

Happy birthday, Mom!
I may have cut the apron strings but
the bond between us will never break.
Thinking of you on your special day.

Sit back, relax and let us make the
cake for once. On your special day you
deserve a rest after all you do for us.
Normal service can be resumed tomorrow!
Happy birthday, Grandma.

I thought you might like something different on
your birthday, so I remembered to write a card
for once. It might not be the luxury cruise you
were hoping for, but it's packed with love!

To our beautiful boy/girl. The day you came into the world was a day we will celebrate for the rest of our lives. Happy birthday, darling.

You're growing up so fast, but you're not too big to have a great big kiss from your Mom. Happy birthday, sweetheart!

Happy birthday! I hope your big day is every bit as special for you as you are for us.

To our little superhero. Have a thrilling, spilling, wowing, powing, dashing, smashing birthday. And don't worry about clearing up afterwards!

Happy birthday to my little girl. I wish you to love life and never stop dreaming. May beauty and happiness surround you today and always!

Happy birthday, darling boy/girl. I may not be able to pick you up any more but you'll always be my precious baby.

Happy birthday, treasure! You will always shine in our hearts.

★

Congratulations on your birthday! Once upon a time there was a world without you in it. How empty it seemed in hindsight. How full it feels today.

I know it's not easy having me
as a brother, but I wouldn't swap
you for the world.
Happy birthday, sis!

When I think about all the years we've
grown up together and things we've
shared, I realize there must be something
very special between us. Have a great
birthday, dear brother!

Throughout my life you have been a
playmate, a soulmate, a friend. But
most of all you've been a brother.
I cherish the day you came into the
world. Happy birthday!

Our special bond was born on this
day and each year it ties us tighter
together. Enjoy your birthday and
know that I'll be toasting the world's
best sister/brother.

To a wonderful aunt/uncle. Thank you for all your kindness and generosity, fun and irreverence. May your birthday be as unforgettable as you are.

As your cousin I feel it's my duty to tell you to have an absolutely marvellous birthday.
Why? Because you deserve it, that's all!

Ahoy there, cousin! I don't want to harpoon about it but here's hoping you have a whale of a time on your birthday.

PARTNERS

To my first, my last, my everything. With love from your soulmate.

Today I'm going to pamper you, spoil you, wait on you and attend to your every whim. Well, why break the habit of a lifetime? Happy birthday!

Millions of interesting people are celebrating their birthday today, but I'm only interested in one – you! Happy birthday, sweetheart!

Sometimes I take it all for granted: your beauty, your charm, your sense of fun, your love. But once a year I'm reminded that your very existence is a miracle. Happy birthday, my angel.

To my lover, my soulmate, my best friend. My love for you grows with each passing year and every birthday marks a new high in our romance. Have a wonderful birthday.

Love is . . . never missing your partner's birthday. Or at least having the good sense to buy a really expensive present when you do! I hope this makes amends. Happy birthday!

Birthdays come and birthdays go, but my love for you remains as constant as the stars. Have a heavenly birthday!

You bring sweetness into my life and set my heart abuzz. Happy birthday, honeybee!

Pussycat – let's curl up by the fire and dream for a while of a purr-fect, pampering birthday.

On your birthday I am reminded that the Earth goes round the Sun and basks in its majestic glow, just as I revolve around you. Happy birthday, you heavenly body you!

A birthday wish for the one I wish was with me now. Though we are far apart, my heart is yours always. Have a great day.

How many cards have I written to you?
How many messages of love have I
penned? Yet still the adoring words flow
from my heart, for my love for you is
a bottomless well. Have the happiest
of birthdays.

Happy birthday! This time last year I
didn't know you, but somewhere in my
heart I was searching for you.
How many people are lucky enough to
find the one they love?

Is that the beating of my heart or have
the party drums started early? It's
your birthday – let's celebrate!

Laurel and Hardy, Bogart and Bacall,
Lennon and McCartney, you and me.
Happy birthday to my irreplaceable
other half!

It's your birthday and I wanted it to be different from every other day we spend together. But then I thought – why? Every other day is perfect. Happy birthday, sweetheart.

★ ★

You gave me love, you gave me children, you gave me strength, you gave me meaning. In return, here's a card. It doesn't seem enough, somehow. With all my love on your birthday!

★ ★

There's nowhere I'd rather be tonight than with you, celebrating your birthday. You mean the world to me and wherever you go, my heart follows.

I'm so glad I remembered your birthday this year, darling. It just shows I'm not as old and decrepit as some people thought. Happy Christmas!

★ ★

It's your birthday and once again I'm reminded how lucky I am that you're mine. Have a wonderful day!

★ ★

Today is your special day and I'm so lucky to be the one spending it with you. You are a truly wonderful partner. Happy birthday!

To my number one, my dinner for two, my holy trinity, my fab four, my five alive, my six of the best, my lucky seven, my eight bells, my cloud nine and my ten out of ten. It's your birthday again – but who's counting?

OTHER CHILDREN

Here's wishing you all the fun a boy/girl could wish for on their birthday and more besides.
Have a cool day!

You're growing up so fast, I can't believe it's your birthday again already! Have a fab day, but slow down, will ya! You're making me feel old.

ॐ

Here's wishing you a day filled with presents, games, friendship and cakes – the perfect recipe for a perfect birthday. Enjoy your special day!

LANDMARKS

Congratulations on reaching double figures. I can't believe it's 10 years since you came to join us and I can't wait to see what you achieve in the next 10. Happy birthday!

Happy 10th birthday. You'll notice more people looking up to you now. Enjoy feeling special. You deserve it.

Happy birthday, sweet 16. You've been waiting so long for this day, but for us it's come round so fast. We hope it brings you all you've been hoping for.

Congratulations on turning 16. May your special day bring you joy and happiness like you've never known before!

You're 18. Go out into the world, carry the lessons you've learnt, the dreams you've always had and the love you've been shown, and light it up as only you can.
But first, have an amazing birthday!

21 isn't the milestone it used to be and there's little left to give you but our love and best wishes as you celebrate this special birthday. May it bring you all the joy and happiness that you've brought us throughout the years.

Here's wishing you a happy and memorable 21st birthday. You have achieved so much in so few years and we are proud to call you our son/ daughter. Congratulations!

They say that life begins at 40.
Here's wishing you a fun and
fabulous start to your new life.
Happy birthday!

Happy 50th birthday. You're halfway
to 100 – way to go! Let's hope the next
50 years bring you as much joy and
happiness as you've given all of us in
your first half-century.

♥ ♥ ♥ ♥ ♥ ♥ ♥ ♥ ♥ ♥ ♥ ♥ ♥ ♥ ♥ ♥ ♥ ♥

Congratulations on 60/70 sensational years.
You have so many wonderful achievements to
look back on, so much to make you proud,
yet so much still to look forward to.
We look forward to it, too.
Many happy returns!

Congratulations on 80 wonderful
years. If I live to be half as gracious,
wise and loved as you, I will
consider it a life well lived.

BELATED

Even though I missed your birthday by a mile, I hope you celebrated it with a smile.

You live life in the fast lane, but I move a little slower. That is why I am a little behind you in celebrating your big day.

A belated birthday wish to one whose charm will always linger, no matter how slow I am to acknowledge it. Happy birthday!

'A diplomat is a man who always remembers a woman's birthday, but never remembers her age.'

Robert Frost

Famous Letters

Ludwig van Beethoven

Upon his death in 1827, a letter was found among the possessions of the great composer Ludwig van Beethoven which revealed a passionate love affair that had remained secret throughout his life. Penned 21 years earlier, the letter refers to his 'immortal beloved'.

My angel, my all, my very self – Only a few words today, and, what is more, written in pencil (and with your pencil) – I shan't be certain of my rooms here until tomorrow; what an unnecessary waste of time is all this. Why this profound sorrow, when necessity speaks – can our love endure without sacrifices, without our demanding everything from one another, can you alter the fact that you are not wholly mine, that I am not wholly yours?– Dear God, look at Nature in all her beauty and set your heart at

*rest about what must be
– Love demands all, and
rightly so, and thus it is
for me with you, for you
with me – but you forget so
easily that I must live for me and for you; if
we were completely united, you would feel
this painful necessity just as little as I do . . .
My heart overflows with a longing to tell you
so many things – Oh – there are moments
when I find that speech is quite inadequate –
Be cheerful – and be for ever my faithful, my
only sweetheart, my all, as I am yours. The
gods must send us everything else, whatever
must and shall be our fate –*

Your faithful Ludwig

Christmas
and
New Year

'He who has not Christmas
in his heart will
never find it under a tree.'

Roy L. Smith

FRIENDS

Christmas is a time for sharing, giving, loving and living. May this Christmas bring you your share of all these things. With love and best wishes.

Though we struggle to see each other throughout the year, you are never far from our thoughts and always in our hearts. Merry Christmas and a Happy New Year!

★ ★

Season's greetings. Your friendship sustains me throughout the year. Here's hoping that next year brings you all the happiness that you bring me.

Christmas reminds us of the value of friendship and the gift of goodwill that we share throughout the year. Here's hoping your Christmas is full of cheer and love.

—∞—

Festive greetings, friends! Thank you for all the fun and laughter we've shared this year. Here's to the next!

The best of the season to you and yours. May Santa bring you all you're hoping for and the New Year fulfil all your wishes.

Here's to the end of a year of joy and friendship, and the beginning of more to come. Merry Christmas and a Happy New Year!

Of all the gifts I get this Christmas, the one I'll cherish most is your valuable friendship. With best wishes for the festive season.

Christmas is a time for carols, presents, feasting and friends. And of these four, the most important is friends. Merry Christmas and a Happy New Year.

Wishing you love, peace and happiness at this special time of year. Our friendship is as constant as the North Star.

As we mark the end of a difficult year,
please know that we are thinking of
you and wishing you all the best.
With love and friendship.

★ ★

This time of year reminds us that
there is always room for hope
in our hearts. May you find the
happiness you deserve.

★ ★

In the depth of the darkest winter,
Christmas brings the brightest light
into our lives: the light of love and
friendship. Here's to you and yours,
with all our love and best wishes.

It may be cold outside, but my
heart is filled with the glow of
friendship. Have a wonderful
Christmas and a very
Happy New Year!

Eat, drink and be merry, for
tomorrow we tidy up! Have
a fantastic Christmas and a
prosperous New Year!

What a year it's been! Here's hoping
that Christmas provides the icing on
the cake and next year sees you build
on your achievements!

**Christmas comes but once a year,
so here's hoping yours is well
worth waiting for. With best
wishes for the festive season.**

*Merry Christmas! Thinking of you
as always at this special time of
year and wishing you all the
best for a very happy and
prosperous New Year.*

Though you may be far away,
you are always close to our
hearts. Have a wonderful
Christmas and a very
Happy New Year!

*May your Christmas
be relaxing, joyful and
contented and may the New
Year bring you peace and
love in abundance. With
all best wishes for the
festive season.*

I hope the holidays bring
you lots of reasons to smile.
Happy Christmas!

FAMILY

To my wonderful Mom at Christmas.
Thank you for your selflessness and love
throughout the year. Now it's your turn
to sit down and be waited on.

★ ★

*Happy Christmas, Dad! May the festive
season take care of you as you take care
of us. With all our love and appreciation.*

**There is no greater gift at Christmas than
the gift of love from a close family.
I am so lucky to have you to share the
festive season with.**

We shall miss you this Christmas but you
will be with us in our hearts and we will
share your happiness from afar.
Merry Christmas, darling!

Merry Christmas to our little angel!
Here's hoping Santa brings you
everything you're hoping for.
You deserve it!

★

At this special time of year, one fire
burns brighter than all others –
the fire of your love.
Merry Christmas, sweetheart!

*Shopping done. Food bought.
Tree decorated. Presents
wrapped. All that's left is
to wrap you up in my love
and wish you a very Merry
Christmas!*

It's Christmas time and there's no one I'd rather spend it with than you. Thank you from the bottom of my heart for making me feel so loved. Happy Christmas!

Merry Christmas to the most wonderful person in the world! Let's celebrate!

★ ★

Merry Christmas and a Happy New Year! We can't wait to see you and share our celebrations with all the family.

To Mrs Santa from Mr Santa. Never mind the presents, your presence is all I need to have a cracker of a Christmas. Ho ho ho!

To my dazzler from your little sugar cookie, may your Christmas sparkle with the glitter of my affection and may the New Year blossom like my love for you. Happy Christmas!

You are the loveliest daughter any parents could wish for and you have filled our home with joy.
Merry Christmas!

BUSINESS ACQUAINTANCES

Best wishes to you and all your staff.
Have a wonderful Christmas and may
the New Year see your business
continue to thrive.

Many thanks for all your trust
and support this year. It has been
a pleasure working with you.
Wishing you a Merry Christmas
and a Happy New Year!

Merry Christmas!
Here's to another year of progress!

Congratulations to everyone on another
impressive year. I look forward to seeing
what you have up your sleeves for the
next! With all best wishes for a Happy
Christmas and a productive New Year.

'Christmas doesn't come from a store, maybe Christmas perhaps means a little bit more....'

How the Grinch Stole Christmas!
by Dr Seuss

Honoré de Balzac

The love affair between French novelist Honoré de Balzac and Polish Countess Eveline Hanska began with an anonymous letter of admiration from her signed 'L'Etrangère' (The Stranger or The Foreigner) in 1832. They met later that year and began a passionate relationship that stood the test of time. However, many barriers stood in the way of their happiness, not the least of which was her husband. At one point, two amorous letters fell into his hands, but Balzac was able to convince him they were part of a complicated joke. When the count died, it turned out Hanska's family did not approve of the writer and this threatened not only her estate but also the inheritance of her daughter. Overcoming all obstacles, they finally married in 1850, just months before Balzac died.

In October 1833 he wrote her this brief letter, brimming with romantic imagery and passion.

*Our love will bloom
always fairer, fresher,
more gracious, because
it is a true love, and because
genuine love is ever increasing.*

*It is a beautiful plant growing from year to
year in the heart, ever extending its palms
and branches, doubling every season its
glorious clusters and perfumes; and, my dear
life, tell me, repeat to me always, that nothing
will bruise its bark or its delicate leaves, that
it will grow larger in both our hearts, loved,
free, watched over, like a life within our life.*

Valentine's Day

'Love is composed
of a single soul
inhabiting
two bodies.'

Aristotle

I love you from the depths of my heart. Your beauty is boundless, your kindness unlimited. What earthly treasures could match the majesty of your soul? Be mine always!

I was lost, a lonely heart, a rudderless ship, a wandering star. You found me and gave me direction. Thank you. With all my love on Valentine's Day.

Neither poetry nor song can do justice to the feelings I have for you. They can only be spoken through silence – a touch, a look, an understanding.

Sometimes I stop and count the years and can't help but wonder how a love can continue to grow, when it felt infinite from the very first day. Happy Valentine's Day!

—⚬—

I dreamed that an angel came into my life, and when I opened my eyes you were there. Please be mine forever!

The way you talk, the way you walk, the way you smile, the way you laugh. Just four reasons why I love you and for every one there are a million more.

I thought I was happy on my own, but now I know what true happiness is I don't ever want to be alone again. Without you my heart is an empty vessel.

With each day that passes I feel closer to you, with each breath you take I love you more. Life holds no fear for me now I have you to look forward to day after day after day.

Stars in the black night, candles in the darkness, a fire in the cold, a whisper in the silence. Your love is my guide, my light, my warmth and my comfort.

My heart is bursting with love for you. I'm so lucky to have you in my life. Yours eternally.

My love for you is deeper than the ocean, stronger than the wind and hotter than the sun. In fact, it's elemental, my dear!

Words cannot do justice to the love I feel for you. All they can do is let you know that a bigger voice is trying to make itself heard. Please go on loving me always.

★ ★

To my loving Valentine. Thank you for being the other half that makes my soul complete. Without you I am nothing. With you, I have all I need.

★ ★

My heart had no purpose until I met you. Now it has love to make it warm, my heart will always beat for you.

They say that love rewards the hopeful and comforts the dreamer.
Be my love and make my hopes and dreams come true!

I see you every morning and my heart skips a beat. Though you may not know me, I dream that one day our hearts will beat as one.
Be my Valentine!

Can you be as beautiful on the inside as you are on the outside?
Be my Valentine and let me know for sure!

ॐ

To my Valentine. I wonder if you notice me as I watch you go by, foolishly gazing after you with hope in my heart. If you do, please turn around, just once, so I know I won't be a fool forever.

'At the touch of
love, everyone
becomes a poet.'

Plato

Mother's Day

'My mother had a great deal of trouble with me, but I think she enjoyed it.'

Mark Twain

MOTHERS

To the one who gave me life, I will always thank you. To the one who gave me direction, I will always turn to you. To the one who gave me love, I will always love you.
Happy Mother's Day!

Would it sound immodest to say what a wonderful job you have done? I hope not, because I mean it purely as a tribute to your love and kindness. Happy Mother's Day!

Happy Mother's Day! The years have been good to you as you've been good to us. You deserve every happiness on your special day.

If all the world had a mother like you, there would be no hatred, no fighting, no strife. I am so lucky to have been raised in your love.

Even the gifts of Mother Nature cannot match the gifts my own mother gave to me – the gifts of life and love. Thanks, Mom. I will love you always.

It's not your birthday or Christmas, so what have you done to deserve all this attention? If I tried to answer that, Mom, I'd need a bigger card!

Today is the day that mothers everywhere receive a little recognition for a job well done. Funny that it should come from the product of their exertions, but who better to know the work that went into creating perfection! Happy Mother's Day!

Thank you, Mom, for always being there when I was alone, for picking me up when I was down and for showing me the path when I was lost.

To a wonderful mother on your special day. Sit down, relax and let us wait on you for a change. You deserve it!

GRANDMOTHERS

Now that I am a mother myself, I know what you went through and my gratitude and admiration know no bounds. I hope it's not too late to say thank you!

All that I am as a mother I learnt from you. If I can be even half as patient, loving and kind, I know I will make my children happy. With love and gratitude on Mother's Day.

★ ★

You may be a grandmother now, but you'll always be a mother to me. Have a great day!

You were so patient and at last you've got your dream – to see me trying to cope with children of my own! Enjoy it, Mom, but please stand by in case of emergencies!

Once a mother, always a mother, and on Mother's Day we remember the heroines of old. Here's to you, Mom, with my eternal gratitude!

I thought motherhood ended when the kids left home. I realize now that it goes on forever and I'm so lucky to have you still looking after me. Thanks a million!

There are mothers, grandmothers and great grandmothers. Seems that mothers just keep getting better and better with age!

PARTNERS

Thank you for giving me
children, for showing them
the way to live and the way to
love. You are a mother in
a million.

**The love you first showed
me is now embracing our
children, too. There are no
limits to the love you give.
Happy Mother's Day.**

To a wonderful wife, a fantastic
friend and magnificent mother.
Thank you for making my
children as lovable as you are.

Parenting is a partnership, but there are some things only a mother can do. Thank you for the amazing job you have done! With all my love on Mother's Day.

I loved you as a girl, I adore you as a mother. Seeing all the gifts you give to our children makes me realize how much you've always given to me. Enjoy your day!

★ ★

Happy Mother's Day! One day a year all the things you do are officially recognized in words.
The rest of the year I just hold you in silent awe!

'A mother's arms
are made of
tenderness and
children sleep
soundly in them.'

Victor Hugo

Famous Letters

Winston Churchill

Britain's great Prime Minister during World War II had an intriguing relationship with his wife, Clementine. Much of their communication took place through letters, the tone of which suggests that if Churchill had a weakness, it was for his wife. This letter was written in January 1935, a period during which Churchill found himself in the political wilderness.

My darling Clemmie,

In your letter from Madras you wrote some words very dear to me, about my having enriched your life. I cannot tell you what pleasure this gave me, because I always feel so overwhelmingly in your debt, if there can be accounts in love . . . What it has been to me to live all these years in your heart and companionship no phrases can convey.

Time passes swiftly, but is it not joyous to see how great and growing is the treasure we have gathered together, amid the storms and stresses of so many eventful and to millions tragic and terrible years?

Your loving husband

Father's Day

'One father is more
than a hundred
schoolmasters.'

George Herbert

FATHERS

On Father's Day we thank you openly for all you've done for us. On every other day we thank you silently. Have a great day, Dad!

Thank you, Dad, for your patience, wisdom, calmness and love. I am so lucky to have you showing me the way in life. With love and appreciation on Father's Day!

★ ★

They say it's impossible being a father: you get all the aggravation and none of the praise. But, Dad, you make it all look so easy! Have a very happy Father's Day!

Dad, you are like a rock in a stormy sea: always there, never shifting, solid and secure. Thank you for keeping my head above water. Happy Father's Day!

—∞—

Happy Father's Day! Thank you for all the time you spend with me playing and teaching and making me laugh. I hope you get to have a sit down today!

To my dear Dad on Father's Day. Take time today to sit down and reflect on the wonderful job you've done. What you have given to us is worth more than all the riches on Earth.

Happy Father's Day, Dad!
Thanks for all your love and
support over the years. Thinking
of you on this special day.

*A good father must be a teacher, an
entertainer, a role model,
a hero, a god. Well, four out
of five ain't bad!
Happy Father's Day, Dad!*

———✺———

This is a day for celebrating fathers and
the amazing job they do. It's also
a day for fathers to have a day off.
Enjoy your break, Dad!

To my Dad, who gives me love and warmth
and strength and comfort every day of my
life. I hope Father's Day brings you all the
happiness you deserve.

GRANDFATHERS

As a father you were benevolent, as a grandfather you are benign. My children are so lucky to feel the same love that I felt. Thanks, Dad. Happy Father's Day!

★ ★

Now that I'm a father, I appreciate more each day the amazing things you did for me, without drama, without recompense, without fail. You deserve all the recognition you get today.

★ ★

Happy Father's Day, Dad! You've taught me that a father never stops being a father, even when his children have children of their own. I am so grateful for your eternal love.

*Dear Dad, it's Father's Day so take the weight off your feet and enjoy watching me try to emulate the brilliant job you did.
It's your time to relax.*

Thanks, Dad, for all your love and support as I've tried to learn the art of parenthood. If I succeed it's because I've been taught by the master.

You may feel freed from fatherly duties now that we're all off your hands with our own fatherly duties to perform, but don't relax too much – we still look to you for inspiration!

I always thought I would make my own rules in life but now that I have children of my own, I find I tell them the same things that you told me. It seems there was more sense in your teaching than I ever realized. Thanks, Dad! Happy Father's Day!

PARTNERS

How well you've risen to the challenge of fatherhood. How naturally you give your love to our child. I always knew you were made for it. Happy Father's Day, darling!

★

Thank you for being the best father a child could have and for being the father of my child. What would we be without you? With all our love on Father's Day.

Parenthood is a partnership and you play your part brilliantly, but today I'm giving you the day off. Have a wonderful Father's Day, sweetheart!

I know that I get most of the credit, but I just want you to know on this special day how much I appreciate the job you do and how glad I am that you're the father of my children. Happy Father's Day!

Three little letters that mean so much
to me: D-A-D. Dependable. Adorable.
Devoted. Without those letters our
children would be poor and I
would be lost. Thank you for being
a wonderful dad!

*Happy Father's Day and
congratulations on a job well done!
I couldn't have done it without you.*

★ ★ ★ ★ ★ ★ ★ ★ ★ ★ ★ ★ ★ ★ ★ ★ ★ ★ ★

**It's been a few years since you changed a diaper
and you don't have to line up for the bathroom
any more, but the fruits of your fatherhood are
out there in the world and your part in their lives
should never be forgotten. Happy Father's Day!**

Sssh! That's the sound of an empty house. It
tells you that your fathering days are done.
Well, until the little darlings run out of money!
Have a relaxing day.

'When I was a boy of fourteen, my father was so ignorant I could hardly stand to have the old man around. But when I got to be twenty-one, I was astonished at how much the old man had learned in seven years.'

Mark Twain

Anniversaries

'A successful marriage requires falling in love many times, always with the same person.'

Mignon McLaughlin

FRIENDS

Congratulations on your anniversary! I hope your day rekindles all the happiness of that magical occasion [x] years ago.

Happy anniversary! What an achievement – to share your life with the same person for so many years, growing closer with each passing day.

Wishing you every happiness on your anniversary. You put a smile on all our faces the day you got married and you continue to make us smile today. Congratulations!

Happy anniversary! You are living proof that the bond of marriage grows stronger year by year, if that bond is built on true love.

❧❧

You are a truly amazing couple and we are in awe of your unwavering devotion. Here's to you and all who seek to emulate you!

Anthony and Cleopatra, Romeo and Juliet, Napoleon and Josephine . . . none of them held it together like you two. Here's to a truly amazing double act!

With love and best wishes on your anniversary. Congratulations on [xx] fabulous years and here's to lots more to come!

PARTNERS

To my Romeo on our anniversary. My passion for you burns like the sun beneath which we made our vows. With love, your Juliet

After all these years you would think I might do away with the whole card thing. But then how would I tell you how gorgeous you are? Happy anniversary!

★ ★

We've made it through our first year! Who'd have thought it? Here's to us! Looks like we're here to stay!

★ ★

Dear Mrs [xxx]. In recognition of your long service in the post of my wife, I wish to recognize your achievement with this short but sincere message of gratitude. Happy anniversary! Mr [xxx].

[x] years ago I met you at the altar, walked you down the aisle and carried you over the threshold. My back's never been the same since! Happy anniversary, darling!

To my one and only on our anniversary. Each year brings more love, so just bring me more years. I can't get enough of you.

❧

Here's to us on our anniversary! Though I say it myself, I think I did rather well marrying you. Let's celebrate my amazing achievement!

❧

To my sweetheart on our anniversary. My memory may not be what it was, but there's one thing I never forget – the day I made you mine. Since then, I've felt like the richest man on Earth.

PARENTS

To Mom and Dad on your anniversary.
Congratulations on [xx] fabulous years together
and all your wonderful little achievements –
which are not so little these days!

Happy anniversary! Another year in the
world's most enduring love story. You
have set us an impeccable example.

**Your marriage is an example to us all
– an inspiring demonstration of love,
faith and fortitude. Here's to many
more anniversaries!**

*Best wishes for a very happy
anniversary. Seeing one's parents
together after all these years is the most
uplifting feeling a person could have.
Have a great day!*

Congratulations on yet another anniversary! You've set a very high bar with your relationship, but given us all the tools with which to match it.

Wishing you joy and happiness on your anniversary. Thank you for creating a happy, secure household and for giving us your love and support without question.

To a wonderful mother and father. Your marriage is a shining example of the power of love and your support for us is testimony to your individual kindness. Happy anniversary!

If people ask me the secret of a good marriage, I need only point them towards you, Mom and Dad. You have taught us that the best things in life are worth working for and that short-term sacrifices yield long-term happiness. With love and gratitude on your anniversary!

GRANDPARENTS

Grandma and Grandpa, you're such a great team: funny, loving and clever. No wonder you've stayed together for all these years. Happy anniversary!

You've set an amazing example with your love for each other and created a family in which we all feel happy and secure. So here's to you on your anniversary – another year of being incredible!

—∿—

Even after all these years you make love look like the most natural thing on Earth. Still holding hands, still kissing, still making each other laugh. I'm sure I don't need to tell you to have a fabulous anniversary!

★ ★

Congratulations on your [xx] anniversary.
What an awesome achievement! We are so
proud of you and grateful for the loving
family you have created.

★ ★

Have a great day on your wedding
anniversary. I'm not sure how many years
it is now and Mom says it's rude to ask,
so I'll just say, Wow – that's brilliant!

*Sending you lots of love and hugs on
your anniversary. You are the best
grandparents anyone could wish for and
it's no surprise you've kept hold of each
other all these years.*

*Here's to you on your anniversary!
I wish we could be there to celebrate
with you, but we'd probably only
slow you down! Have a ball!*

CHILDREN

Congratulations on your anniversary! Seeing you in a happy, secure relationship is the best gift a parent could have. Enjoy your day!

ॐ

Here's to another year of marriage! See, it's not so bad, is it? In fact, you make it look easy. Have a wonderful anniversary!

Wishing you all the best on your anniversary. In a few short years you have become old hands at this marriage thing and seeing you together brings joy to our hearts.

'*My most brilliant achievement was my ability to be able to persuade my wife to marry me.*'

Winston Churchill

King Henry VIII

The courtship between the Tudor king, Henry VIII, and his second wife, Anne Boleyn, is one of history's most famously torrid love affairs. This letter, written by Henry as he sought to gain Anne's commitment prior to his divorce from Katherine of Aragon, shows his uncertainty about her feelings for him and his desperation to win her love.

To My Mistress,

Because the time seems very long since I heard concerning your health and you, the great affection I have for you has induced me to send you this bearer, to be better informed of your health and pleasure, and because, since my parting from you, I have been told that the opinion in which I left you is totally changed, and that you would not come to court either with your mother, if you could, or in any other manner; which report, if true, I cannot sufficiently marvel at, because I am sure that I have since never done any thing to

*offend you, and it seems a
very poor return for the
great love which I bear
you to keep me at
a distance both from the
speech and the person of
the woman that I esteem
most in the world: and if you
love me with as much affection as I hope you
do, I am sure that the distance of our two
persons would be a little irksome to you,
though this does not belong so much to the
mistress as to the servant.*

*Consider well, my mistress, that absence
from you grieves me sorely, hoping that it
is not your will that it should be so; but if I
knew for certain that you voluntarily desired
it, I could do no other than mourn my ill-
fortune, and by degrees abate my great folly.*

*And so, for lack of time, I make an end of this
rude letter, beseeching you to give credence
to this bearer in all that he will tell you
from me.*

Written by the hand of your entire Servant,

HR

Engagements

*'And when Love speaks,
the voice of all the gods
Makes heaven drowsy
with the harmony.'*

From *Love's Labour's Lost* by
William Shakespeare

FAMILY

What a thrill for us to learn that our own beautiful daughter/ handsome son is to be married! Congratulations and thank you for making us such proud parents.

Thank you, darling, for telling us the wonderful news of your engagement to [name]. You have made an excellent choice (as has he/she) and we are delighted for you both.

Hey! I hear I'm to get a new brother/sister-in-law. Fantastic news! I know you'll be very happy together and I can't wait for the wedding.

Very well done on getting [name] to agree to marry you. That really is some achievement! In all honesty, I think he/she has made a very astute choice and I wish you both every happiness for the future. Cheers, bro/sis!

Fantastic news about your engagement! I don't feel I'm losing a brother so much as gaining a really rather gorgeous sister. Thanks and well done!

So you've finally decided to tie the knot. I didn't want to say anything before, but now I can . . . it's about time! We've been waiting years for this moment and now it's arrived I can't tell you how thrilled we are. Congratulations!

FRIENDS

We heard the news and had to write immediately. Congratulations! We've always thought you made a lovely couple and now you're going to make a lovely married couple.

Fantastic news about your engagement! Congratulations, both of you. It's not often that two people make a brilliant decision at the same time, but you always were exceptional!

I was looking for an excuse to wear my wedding hat again and now I have it. I'm so pleased for you both and I can't wait to see you tie the knot.

How delighted we were to hear your exciting news! Finding your partner for life is a truly amazing experience and we share your happiness.

I heard you finally plucked up the courage to propose and [name] had the good sense to accept. That's the kind of news I like to hear. Congratulations, both of you! You'll make a wonderful couple.

★ ★

Here's to you on your engagement! We look forward eagerly to the wedding when we can raise a glass to you in person and toast your health and happiness.

I do love a good wedding and yours will be one of the best ever! You are a very special couple and your love is clear for all to see. Thank you for giving us all something to celebrate.

Wow! You're engaged. It seems like only yesterday we were starting school together. Congratulations to you both, and thanks for putting the pressure on me!

It gives me so much joy to see you and [name] together. You will make a truly gorgeous couple and you will always have love by your side.

So, not such a hopeless case after all! Congratulations on your engagement from your oldest friend. How long have I got to write my speech?

Fantastic to hear you've got engaged. As friends you are wonderful, as husband and wife you'll be unstoppable! Wishing you every happiness for your nuptials and a long and loving life together.

'How silver-sweet sound lovers' tongues by night, Like soft music to attending ears.'

From *Romeo and Juliet*
by William Shakespeare

Wedding

'My advice to you is get married: if you find a good wife you'll be happy; if not, you'll become a philosopher.'

Socrates

FAMILY

When we got married our dream was to have children and see them grow up to be happy, healthy adults. Today that dream is fulfilled and we couldn't be more excited. You will make a wonderful couple and we look forward to seeing you fulfil your own dreams.

★ ★

I'm so glad that you are embarking on the journey of marriage together. Between the two of you I see a love that is rare and strong, a love that can conquer all. I want you to know that I am so proud of you and will always love you.

Wishing you love on your wedding day, as you and [name] prepare for your life together as husband and wife. Thank you for all the proud, happy moments you have given us. I don't think you can begin to know just how many of those there have been, but today they all come together in the happiest and proudest moment of all. We hope your day goes beautifully and we wish you all our love for a long and fruitful marriage.

What you have done today, [name] and [name], is a truly wonderful thing and we are immensely proud of you. You are two gems, who together form a treasure that makes the world a richer place. Your love does not just touch each other, it touches all who come into your presence. Congratulations on your wedding day!

Congratulations on your wedding! This day has come round so fast it's left us breathless. Maybe it's the excitement we feel at seeing you so happy together, and for the joys your marriage may hold. You are a great couple and we hope your special day brings you as much joy as you have brought us in making it happen.

Today is your special day. As we eagerly await the ceremony that will see you become man and wife, I'd like to take this opportunity to tell you how proud I am to be your brother/sister. I am honored that you have asked me to play this role in your wedding. I will do my best to ensure that today goes as smoothly and merrily as possible and that you get to enjoy it as thoroughly as you deserve. Congratulations!

May your lives be a great adventure. May your battles be fought together side by side and let there be joy and abundance.

★ ★

We wish you a world of happiness on your wedding day. May your married life be everything that you imagined and more.

★ ★

My greatest wish for the two of you is that through the years your love for each other will so deepen and grow, that years from now, you will look back on this day, your wedding day, as the day you only started to really love each other.

FRIENDS

A wedding is a start of togetherness
. . . of walks in the rain, basking in
the sunshine, shared meals, caring
for one another and sensing the love
that a marriage carries.

**I have always had this feeling that
you were meant for each other. I'm
so glad to see you guys together.
Congratulations! I hope you remain this
happy for the rest of your lives.**

*When a friend gets married it's a happy
day. When two friends get married it's a
busy day. When two friends get married
to each other it's the best day of my
life! I can't wait to see you together as
husband and wife and I will love you
even more now you are one.*

Today's the day, as they say! You're finally getting married. My money was on next June but hey, I don't mind being wrong if it means seeing you two finally do the decent thing! Have a great day and a very happy life together.

Here's to you on your wedding day! Rest assured that we will be celebrating loud and long. You are a truly great friend and we are delighted that you have found love and happiness with [name]. Wishing you all the best for your life together as husband and wife.

I just wanted to say one last thing before you quit the single life. We've been friends for many years. We've lived together, laughed together, worked together and played together. We've been inseparable and I thought we could never be happier. But I was wrong. Today is the happiest day of your life and mine. I am so glad for you.

Wishing you the very best of luck on your wedding day. May it bring you every happiness and may your life together be blessed with love always.

★ ★ ★ ★ ★ ★ ★ ★ ★ ★ ★ ★ ★ ★ ★ ★ ★ ★ ★ ★

Congratulations on your wedding! We can't wait to see you and we look forward to meeting [name]. Here's hoping the sun shines and you have a wonderful day!

Looking forward to your wedding day. Congratulations to both of you and may your life together be a merry-go-round of joy and laughter!

I am overjoyed by the news that you're getting married and I would be delighted to come to the wedding. Thank you so much for inviting me. I wish you luck with the planning and I hope the day fulfils all your dreams.

We're so excited to be seeing you on your wedding day. We're sure the day will be truly memorable and we look forward to meeting your new bride/husband.

Thank you for inviting us to your wedding. We wouldn't miss it for the world. Here's looking forward to a very happy occasion and a life full of laughter, happiness and the patter of tiny feet!

Thank you so much for the invitation to your wedding. I'm sorry that we won't be able to attend, but promise to be there in spirit. We'll raise a glass to you both to toast your future together.

To the happy couple to be, many thanks for inviting us to join you in celebrating your marriage. We would love to be there but unfortunately circumstances prevent us. We will be thinking of you on the day, and send our best wishes for a lovely wedding and a very happy life together.

With deep regret I have to decline your kind invitation to attend your wedding. It would have been a real thrill to share in your happy day. I will raise a glass or two to you as you begin your life together. With all best wishes now and for the future.

'I have great hopes that we shall love each other all our lives as much as if we had never married at all.'

Lord Byron

Mark Twain

One of the greatest American writers of all time, the author of *The Adventures of Tom Sawyer* and *The Adventures of Huckleberry Finn* was a renowned wit and genius with words. This brief letter to his future wife, Olivia Langdon, written a year before their marriage in 1869, when he was 33 and she ten years his junior, shows his sincere side; but it still contains that glint of humor characteristic of Twain's writing style.

*Out of the depths of my
happy heart wells a great
tide of love and prayer for
this priceless treasure that is
confided to my life-long keeping.*

*You cannot see its intangible waves as
they flow towards you, darling, but in
these lines you will hear, as it were, the
distant beating of the surf.*

Births

*'It is the nature
of babies to be
in bliss.'*

Deepak Chopra

FAMILY

Many congratulations on a successful birth and thank you for making us proud grandparents! We will cherish our role, just as we cherished the role of parenthood, though this time we look forward to getting all the pleasure and none of the hardship. That's your job!

Fantastic news! Well done to you both. We are so proud of you and thrilled at the prospect of meeting our new grandson/granddaughter.

Congratulations on the birth of your son. We are so very pleased for you both and so proud to have become grandparents again! May he bring you all the joy that you brought us.

Congratulations on the birth of your daughter. We can't wait to meet her.

We just wanted to put in writing how delighted we are that you have become a father/mother. This is a momentous occasion and we are so pleased for you. Tell him his Grandma and Grandpa are itching to meet him and we hope he will remember to be at his best and to mind his manners!

Fabulous news about the new baby, sis. I'm so proud of you and I trust you and [baby] are well, and that [father] survived the ordeal without too much trauma! I can't wait to see you and meet my new niece/nephew.

Congratulations on becoming a father. If you're half as good at that as you are at being a brother, your new baby will have a wonderful childhood. I hope you are all well and that [mother] has recovered from the birth and is enjoying her new treasure. I look forward to seeing you with babe in arms.

So pleased to hear the baby came safe and sound. You're an old hand at this now, but I know you'll be just as thrilled with your new arrival as you were with your first. I certainly am and I'm very excited at meeting my new niece/nephew.

Congratulations on your new addition to the family. Look after each other and enjoy your time at home together.

★ ★

You've done it! Many congratulations on the birth of your son/daughter. It's been so exciting watching you grow over the last few months and I'm delighted that the birth went ahead without a hitch. I hope you get lots of joy from your new bundle.

★ ★

I let out a loud whoop when I heard your fantastic news and had to spend the next 10 minutes explaining to everyone in the office! I'm so proud to tell everyone that I'm an uncle/aunt.

You're a mom! I'm an uncle!! This is the best news I've heard all year and I can't stop telling people. Anyone would think I'd given birth myself! I'm so proud of you, sis, and I'm so looking forward to holding my new nephew/niece.

Thank you for the wonderful news and congratulations on your new arrival. I'm bowled over at becoming an auntie. Enjoy your new baby over the coming days and make sure you get some sleep!

Congratulations on your wonderful news! This is such an exciting time for all the family. I hope you are finding the time to enjoy your new baby between all the visits. I want you to know how proud I am to be an aunt/uncle and that I will always cherish your new addition to the family.

FRIENDS

> *We heard the fantastic news and wanted to write to say how thrilled we are for you both. You will make terrific parents. With all our best wishes for your life ahead with your new baby.*

I heard the stork arrived. Congratulations! It's a wonderful achievement and such an exciting time. When you look at your baby, nothing else matters in the world. I hope the euphoria lasts a lifetime!

★ ★

Many congratulations on the birth of your son/daughter. We were so pleased when we heard the news. We hope you have now recovered from the birth and are enjoying some peaceful time with your baby. You've earned it!

Congratulations on the new addition to your family! We were so pleased to hear that the birth went well and we wish you every happiness with your new son/daughter.

Wonderful to hear about your new baby. Many congratulations to Mom and Dad and we look forward to meeting the little boy/girl very soon. With all our best wishes.

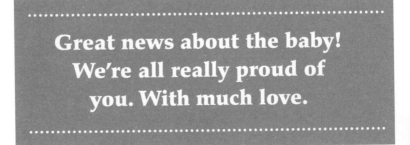

Great news about the baby! We're all really proud of you. With much love.

I heard the stork brought you a little present in the night. What a wonderful feeling, to look into the eyes of your offspring. You must be brimming with happiness, as are we. Congratulations!

Pop the champagne, there's a new life in the world! How fantastic for you and your family. You have every reason to feel proud. Congratulations!

Congratulations on becoming a dad! I know it means there'll have to be a few changes but I'm sure you're up to it and will make a wonderful father. With all our love and best wishes.

Congratulations on becoming a mother! What you've achieved is something remarkable and brave and you deserve all the happiness that comes with a new baby. And well done to dad, too! We look forward to seeing you and your new arrival very soon.

A few words of advice . . . sleep whenever you get the chance, eat as much as you like, allow others to wait on you hand and foot and enjoy the euphoria of the first weeks. Congratulations and best wishes!

Now that you're a father, you may be needing a bit of advice from time to time. Let me tell you, there is only one rule: do whatever you're told to do whenever you're told to do it! The rest is plain sailing. Well done. We're proud of you.

*'Men are often
bad, but babies
never are.'*

Louisa May Alcott

Milestones

'Every day is a new beginning, and every sunset is merely the latest milestone on a voyage that never ends.'

Ronald Reagan

CHRISTENING

Congratulations on the christening of [child's name] and thank you for the honor of making me a godparent. I will do everything in my power to ensure my duties to [child's name] are fulfilled and to be a constant support for you as parents.

Today is a special day for you, for [baby's name] and for me. I take the responsibilities that come with being a godparent very seriously and I am humbled that you have chosen me for this role. With love and best friendship always.

CONFIRMATION/BAR MITZVAH

Congratulations on your confirmation/
coming of age. May your faith
forever sustain you and inspire you
to great things.

Best wishes on the occasion of your
confirmation/bar mitzvah. This is
a proud day for you and all of us
who know and love you.
May God bless and protect you
now and forever.

*Our thoughts are with you on your
special day. Congratulations on
achieving this milestone and on all
your accomplishments. We look
forward to many more to come.*

NEW SCHOOL

Today you start your new school. May this be the beginning of a wonderful adventure that will fill you with new knowledge and experiences. We are so very proud of you.

Wishing you the best of luck in your new school. This is a major milestone in anyone's life and we hope you take to it like a duck to water. With love and pride.

I just know you're going to have the time of your life at your new school. Embrace every opportunity that comes your way, ask questions, soak up knowledge, make lots of friends and enjoy every minute. We will be proud of you always.

Good luck in your new school. Work hard, play hard and fulfil your undoubted potential.

EXAMS

Good luck with your exams. We know you have worked extremely hard and you deserve to do very well. We'll be rooting for you all the way!

Thinking of you as you begin your exams. I hope all the hard work and preparation pays off and that you get the grades you deserve. Whatever happens, I'm proud of you!

Congratulations on your exam results. It must be great to know you've got your reward after all that hard work. Well done!

★ ★

Brilliant news about your exams! We always knew you had it in you, but those grades are something else!

GRADUATION

Wonderful news about your graduation!
Congratulations! You should be extremely
proud of your achievement. It will stand you in
good stead as you take your many gifts
into the world.

Congratulations on your degree! You have
worked very hard and your success is well-
deserved. We are so pleased for you and
wish you all the best for your future career,
whatever you choose to do.

**Congratulations on your excellent
degree result! Now you have the world
at your feet and we have no doubt that
you will make it a better place. Enjoy
your celebrations!**

*Well done on passing your degree!
Another milestone in a journey full of
accomplishments. We look forward to
seeing where life takes you next.*

NEW JOB

Good luck in your new job. I know you will make an outstanding success of it and I am so glad that this opportunity has come your way.

Congratulations on landing the job! We always knew you had a lot to give if only you were given the chance, and now that door has opened. Grasp the opportunity with both hands and don't look back!

Sending you our love and best wishes as you start your new job. We are confident that you will be a roaring success and the promotions will follow thick and fast.

Great news about the new job. We knew your perseverance and patience would get their reward in the long run and this looks like a wonderful opportunity. We hope you are very happy in your new role.

RETIREMENT

Wow! I didn't think you were old enough to retire! You must be so excited to reach this milestone and although I'll be sorry to see you go, I share your joy. Have a wonderful retirement and do all those things you've dreamed about.

Congratulations on your retirement! Your working days are done, and now begins the fun. We hope this new era in your life brings you happiness and fulfilment beyond your wildest dreams.

★ ★ ★ ★ ★ ★ ★ ★ ★ ★ ★ ★ ★ ★ ★ ★ ★ ★ ★

What's this about retirement? You told me you were 21! Well, I always thought you were mature for your years, but now I know the truth. I will miss you, but the thought of you in your garden will always bring a smile to my face.
Good luck!

'Even though the Lord's pay isn't very high, his retirement program is, you might say, out of this world.'

George Foreman

Famous Letters

Napoleon Bonaparte

The great French general and emperor was renowned for his prowess on the field of battle but he was also a master of letter writing. The subject of many of his estimated 75,000 missives was his wife, Josephine, to whom he wrote this famous letter in the December before their marriage in 1796.

I wake filled with thoughts of you. Your portrait and the intoxicating evening which we spent yesterday have left my senses in turmoil. Sweet, incomparable Josephine, what a strange effect you have on my heart! Are you angry? Do I see you looking sad? Are you worried? . . . My soul aches with sorrow, and there can be no rest for you lover; but is there still more in store for me when, yielding to the profound feelings which overwhelm me, I draw from your lips, from your heart a

love which consumes me with fire? Ah! It was last night that I fully realized how false an image of you your portrait gives!

You are leaving at noon; I shall see you in three hours.

Until then, mio dolce amor, a thousand kisses; but give me none in return, for they set my blood on fire.

Achievements

'Optimism is the
faith that leads to
achievement. Nothing
can be done without
hope and confidence.'

Helen Keller

GENERAL

We heard your wonderful news. You must be so proud of what you have achieved, as are all of us who know and love you. You have worked so hard and overcome so many obstacles – this really is a fitting reward. Well done!

★ ★

Some are born great, some achieve greatness and some have greatness thrust upon them. Having known and lived with you from birth, you definitely fall into the middle category! I'm so proud of your achievement.

Fantastic news about the promotion! If you're looking for ways to spend the extra pay, I've got a few ideas we could discuss.

We always knew there was something special about you, but this really is a remarkable achievement. Through passion, commitment, perseverance and integrity you have succeeded where thousands fail, and we feel privileged to know you.

I'm sorry to say I've been telling everyone I know that you are a friend of mine. I couldn't resist basking in your reflected glory for a while. I am so excited by your achievement, it's almost as if I did it myself! You are amazing.

PROMOTION

Congratulations on your promotion! I knew you would do well in that job from the start and this is a fitting reward for all your hard work.

Just heard about your promotion. Great news and thoroughly deserved. We must catch up soon so I can buy you a drink.

Congratulations on your latest step up the career ladder. I hope that management suits you and you are able to inspire your staff to the same heights that you have achieved. Well done!

AWARDS

So the judges made the right choice, I hear. Congratulations! I know you're not bothered about awards, but this is recognition for the excellent work you do and you should feel proud of what you've achieved.

Congratulations on being awarded such a prestigious prize. What an honor! You thoroughly deserve it and I hope it opens the door to further recognition in future.

★ ★ ★ ★ ★ ★ ★ ★ ★ ★ ★ ★ ★ ★ ★ ★ ★ ★ ★

I was delighted to hear you won the prize! You have worked so hard and followed your heart and this is recognition of your courage and brilliance. Congratulations!

WINNING

Congratulations on winning your race! I was so proud watching you trying so hard, I was in tears when you crossed the line. You are a brave competitor and you deserve your prize.

Very well done on coming first! You have put in so much hard work and made so many sacrifices preparing for this, I am delighted that it's all paid off. Enjoy the euphoria!

Well done on your recent win! It must have been immensely satisfying and was certainly thoroughly deserved. Congratulations!

*'Happiness lies
in the joy of
achievement
and the thrill of
creative effort.'*

Franklin D. Roosevelt

Get Well Soon

'I enjoy convalescence.
It is the part that makes
the illness worthwhile.'

George Bernard Shaw

FAMILY ILLNESS – MINOR

I just wanted to say what an amazing patient you've been. I know you've been feeling rotten, but you haven't grumbled about it once. Thank you. I hope you feel better soon.

It's no fun being ill, but it helps to know you're being properly cared for. I also wanted you to know that I'm here if there's anything you need.
Get well soon!

You poor thing, you must be in a lot of pain. Make sure you take it easy and do all you need for a speedy recovery. Don't worry about anything else.

Ouch! That must have been painful. I hope you're going to let us look after you until you're fit to get around again. Don't feel you have to battle through this on your own. Just pick up the phone. We're here to help.

How brave you've been since your accident! We're all so proud of the way you've coped with the pain and disappointment and delighted that you're recovering so fast.

FRIENDS' ILLNESS – MINOR

I heard you were feeling poorly and I wanted to send my commiserations. It's no fun being ill in this weather, but you have a wonderful family around you and I know they will have you back on your feet in no time.

★ ★

A quick note to let you know we're thinking of you and miss you very much. Hurry up and get well soon! We need you back.

Life around here just isn't the same without you. I do hope you make a speedy recovery and come back soon to brighten up my life.

I was very sorry to hear you have been unwell recently. It is no fun being ill and I hope you'll feel better soon. Take as much time as you need to make a full recovery and I will look forward to seeing you fully restored!

We hear you've been feeling below par and wanted to send you our love and best wishes. Get well soon! We're all missing you terribly!

We were all pleased to hear your operation was a success. That must be such a relief for you. Now you can concentrate on getting back to full health once again. We wanted to let you know we're thinking of you.

Commiserations on your accident. It sounded painful! We all send our love and best wishes for a speedy recovery.

Best wishes from all of us for a quick return to health. It's hard to imagine you being stuck in a hospital bed for too long. Get well soon!

MAJOR ILLNESS

I'm so sorry that you're suffering and I pray that you will feel better soon. Please let me know if there is anything I can do to help you through this illness. With all our support, you'll be back on your feet in no time.

You've been so good at looking after us all of our lives, now it's our turn to take care of you. We are here to support you through this and we know you have the strength to beat it. Keep on taking the medicine, and you'll be back on form in next to no time.

★ ★

You have been so brave in the way you've coped since your accident and I am sure that you will go on to make a full recovery. Meanwhile, I want you to know that I am here to give you help when you need it, company when you want it and love always. Get well soon!

I know that sympathy is the last thing you need, but I wanted you to know that we are all thinking of you and wishing you every success with your fight back to health. You have the strength to overcome anything and we look forward to seeing you back in action very soon.

I was so sorry to hear of your illness. My heart goes out to you and your family and if there is some little thing I can do to ease your burden, I would be only too pleased. Stay strong and you will beat this.

Your courage is an inspiration to us all. We know that you have been going through a very difficult time but you have kept a brave face throughout. The great thing is that the love of your friends and family will give you the strength to make a full recovery. We are all rooting for you.

We hope you find it comforting to know that we're all thinking of you and wishing you a speedy recovery from your illness. We miss you and hope to have you back with us very soon.

———⁓———

I heard that you've been ill, but are now over the worst of it and starting to feel human again. I hope you get your strength and energy back before too long and can start enjoying life again.

We just wanted you to know that we are all thinking of you as you prepare for your operation. We were so sorry to hear what you've been going through and we pray for a successful outcome so you can start getting back to full health. We care deeply about you and wish you the very best of luck.

'*Love begins by taking care of the closest ones – the ones at home.*'

Mother Teresa

Famous Letters

Abraham Lincoln

The president who led America out of the Civil War was a master of succinctness and this letter is a shining example. It was written to a Mrs Lydia Bixby, whose five sons had been reported killed in action during the war. In fact, it turned out that three of them survived, but at the time of writing Lincoln understood that the widow had lost her entire family.

Dear Madam,

I have been shown in the files of the War Department a statement of the Adjutant General of Massachusetts that you are the mother of five sons who have died gloriously on the field of battle.

I feel how weak and fruitless must be any word of mine which should attempt to beguile you from the grief of a loss so overwhelming.

*But I cannot refrain
from tendering you the
consolation that may be
found in the thanks of the
Republic they died to save.*

*I pray that our Heavenly Father may assuage
the anguish of your bereavement, and leave
you only the cherished memory of the loved
and lost, and the solemn pride that must be
yours to have laid so costly a sacrifice upon
the altar of freedom.*

Yours, very sincerely and respectfully,

A. Lincoln

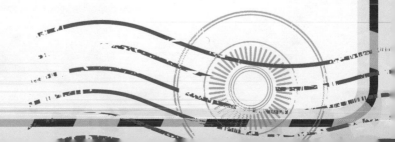

Sympathy

'Give sorrow words;
the grief that does not
speak knits up the o'er
wrought heart and bids
it break.'

From *Macbeth* by
William Shakespeare

CLOSE FRIENDS AND RELATIONS

I wanted to let you know that we all share your grief, tempered by many wonderful memories of a very special person. In time you will find that the sadness fades and happy memories take its place. Until that happens, we, your friends, are here for you. Please stay in touch.

As I write to you with my condolences, my head is filled with images of [name of deceased] and the joy he/she brought to all of us who were lucky enough to know and love him/her. He/she was a truly special person and we are all deeply sorry for your loss.

There are no words to adequately express the sadness I felt when I heard about the death of [name of deceased]. He/she was an example to us all. I will never know another like [name of deceased] and my thoughts are with you at this difficult time.

It feels like the world has stopped in honor of a great man/woman. We were so sorry to hear about [name of deceased] and our thoughts are with you at this time. We hope you may be able to take some comfort from the many tributes we know will be paid to him/her, by those who also held him/her in such high regard.

As long as the memories remain, they will inspire new life. I hope that time will heal your grief and help you to accept the sad passing of your father/ mother as a step on a journey that never ends.

We were very sad to learn of the death of [name of deceased]. He/she was such a fun-loving person whose mission in life seemed to be to make others laugh. We will always remember him/her fondly and we are thinking of you in your time of grieving.

I was so sorry to hear of your tragic loss. I cannot begin to imagine the pain you must be feeling. [name of deceased] was a sweet, loving child, who lit up the hearts of all of us. You and your family are in our prayers.

I wanted to express my sadness at learning of [name of deceased]'s passing. He/she was always very kind to me and I have many fond memories of things we did together. He/she will be missed and my thoughts are with you at this difficult time.

I heard your sad news and wanted to write to convey my sympathies and let you know that I am here for you if you need me, as I'm sure are so many of your other friends. I thought the world of [name of deceased] and will always remember him/her with the deepest of affection.

I was so sorry to hear that [name of deceased] passed away yesterday. He/she was a dear friend and has left us with many happy memories. My heart goes out to you at this difficult time and I share your grief for a man/woman who lit up our lives with laughter, kindness and love.

Words cannot express my sorrow on learning of [name of deceased]'s sad passing. It came as a great shock to learn of his/her sudden death, and I bitterly regret not having contacted him/her in recent times. Now that this terrible unexpected event has occurred, it brought home to me the importance of friendship. We must make sure that we stay in touch.

DISTANT ACQUAINTANCES

I was sorry to hear that you recently lost [name of deceased] after his/her battle with illness. My thoughts and prayers are with you in your time of grieving, but I hope there will be some relief in knowing that [name of deceased] is not suffering any more.

I was sorry to hear about the loss of [name of deceased].
He/she was much respected by all of us and will be sorely missed.

We are writing to express our sadness at the death of [name of deceased] and to convey our sympathies for your loss. We know you have people around you who will share your grief and help you through this difficult time.

News reached us today of the sad passing of [name of deceased] and I wanted to send my condolences. [name of deceased] was a fine man/woman and will be sorely missed.

I am so sorry about the tragic death of your son/daughter. I can't imagine the pain you are going through and I can only offer the condolences of someone who never knew [name of deceased], but was deeply moved by his/her story. My thoughts are with you and all your family.

★ ★

Please accept our sympathy and best wishes in your time of grieving. We hope you find comfort among your friends and family and cherish the memories of your dear husband/wife.

I am writing to tell you how sorry I am that your husband/wife has passed away. The pain of losing someone so close can seem unbearable, but I hope the love of all your many friends will bring some consolation. My thoughts are with you at this difficult time.

We have just learned that [name of deceased] passed away and are very saddened by the news. Our recollections of [name of deceased] are of an intelligent, warm and generous man/woman who had time for everyone, regardless of how busy he/she was. The world has lost one of its best and he/she will be greatly missed.

So sorry to hear about your grandma. I know she had been ill for some time, but I was very sad to hear of her passing. [name of deceased] It was always lovely to chat whenever we met. She was such a warm and lovely lady. I will miss her greatly.

I heard that your father passed away after a long battle with [illness]. He was a brave man and a fighter, but he can rest now; the suffering is over. He was always very kind to me in times of crisis and I have much to thank him for. Please accept my sympathy and best wishes.

'You don't know who is important to you until you actually lose them.'

Mahatma Gandhi

Goodbyes

'Parting is such sweet sorrow.'

From *Romeo and Juliet* by William Shakespeare

LEAVING WORK

Sorry you're leaving. It's been fantastic working with you and the place won't be the same when you're gone. Good luck in your next venture!

We will miss you when you're gone. Your presence around the office has been invaluable these last few years and it will be hard filling your shoes. Best of luck!

I can't believe you're leaving! Who's going to make me laugh in the coffee break and sing for me when the afternoon's dragging by? Working here will never be the same again.

Good luck in your new job! You have been a terrific colleague and a valued friend and I will miss you when you're gone. Keep in touch!

Nothing lasts forever, but I rather hoped it might in your case. I have loved every minute of working with you and always dreaded the idea that you might seek new challenges elsewhere. I always suspected you would, though, as you have so much to offer. Carry on up the greasy pole, but always be my friend.

A heartfelt 'thank you' for all your hard work. You have been a highly valued colleague and I appreciate everything you have done for the department. Good luck in your new role!

★ ★

I'm sorry you're leaving. You have been inspiring as a boss and a real pleasure to work for. I wish you every success in your new job.

The very best of luck as you leave us
for pastures new. While we're sorry to
see you go, we know you will thrive
in your new role and will keep an eye
on your progress. Thanks for all your
hard work!

*So sorry to see you go. This marks the end
of an era and I know a lot of people will
miss you about the place. I hope you don't
have to wait too long to find another job
and I wish you all the best.*

**What a shame you're leaving! This
company needs more people like you,
not fewer, and I can't see how they will
replace you. Wishing you the very
best of luck!**

*Goodbye and good luck! I hope you are
happy in your new job and I look forward
to hearing about your progress.*

RETIREMENT

Good luck on your retirement. You have been part of the furniture at this company for many years and you will be impossible to replace. We will all miss you and we hope you'll come back to say hello now and then.

★ ★ ★ ★ ★ ★ ★ ★ ★ ★ ★ ★ ★ ★ ★ ★ ★ ★ ★ ★

Congratulations on your retirement. I have enjoyed every minute of working with you and it will seem very strange once you're gone. Enjoy relaxing and I hope you fulfil those dreams I've been hearing about for all these years.

★ ★ ★ ★ ★ ★ ★ ★ ★ ★ ★ ★ ★ ★ ★ ★ ★ ★ ★ ★

We will miss you when you're gone but we wish you every happiness in your retirement. You've earned it!

This place just won't be the same without you. Someone said you've been here longer than the carpets, and that's saying something! I feel privileged to have known and worked with you, so thank you. With love and best wishes for a very happy retirement.

MOVING AWAY

What an exciting time for you – moving to a new town and a new life. I hope everything works out just as you planned, but remember we will always be here if you decide to come back. Don't be a stranger!

I'm sad that you're moving away but I'm also excited for you. I will miss our chats and time spent in your company, but I hope you settle in fast in your new town and I'll always be just a phone call away if you need me.

I heard you're moving away and I just wanted to say goodbye. I will miss seeing your smiling face each morning, but I know this is a golden opportunity for you so I hope you take it with both hands and it works out well. With very best wishes.

Good luck in your new home. I know this is an important move for you and I really hope it works out, although a part of me wishes you were staying right here. You are a dear friend and I will make sure we keep in touch.

Wishing you the best of luck with your move to [location]. I hope you settle in quickly and find comfort and happiness in your new home.

★ ★

Best wishes for the big move! Keep in touch and come back to see us as soon as you get the chance.

EMIGRATING

Good luck as you embark upon your new life in [country]. It is a brave decision and I know there are many of us who will miss you when you're gone. I hope you find your feet quickly and I'm sure the locals will take to you just as we did and welcome you with open arms. Keep in touch and come back and see us sometime.

I almost wish I could be going with you as you pack your bags for [country]. I will be thinking of you and hope one day to come and visit you in your new home. Take care and good luck!

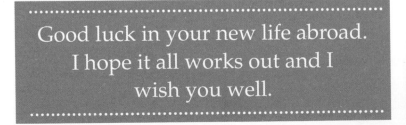

Good luck in your new life abroad. I hope it all works out and I wish you well.

The house is sold, the boxes are packed and all that remains is to say your goodbyes. Let me tell you that I will shed tears. You have been such a good friend to me and I will miss you desperately. Promise to come back and see me at the first opportunity and I will always be waiting on the end of the phone. With love and best wishes in your new home.

You are about to embark on a fabulous adventure and I would like to wish you well as you set sail for [country]. I will miss you, but the world is a smaller place these days and this could be the excuse I need to finally get out and see more of it! Keep in touch!

You're moving away, but that doesn't mean you're moving out of my life. It's only a few hundred miles and we all need to travel now and again. So keep in touch and let's make sure we see each other again soon. With love and best wishes.

TRAVELLING

Bon voyage! Here's wishing you all the very best for your travels. I hope you see some amazing sights and have some wonderful adventures.

I am so excited for you as you prepare to embark on your great adventure. I hope the world is ready for you! Have a fantastic time and I look forward to hearing all about it when you return.

Have a wonderful time on your travels and take good care of yourself. I will miss you while you're gone and will count the seconds until you are back here in my arms.

Good luck on your exciting adventure around the world. I know you will have the time of your life and won't want to come home, but we will all be waiting with open arms when you finally do. Take care and have a brilliant time!

'Gone – flitted away,
Taken the stars from
the night and the sun
From the day!
Gone, and a cloud in
my heart.'

Alfred Lord Tennyson

Famous Letters

Marlon Brando

The great American actor was on a flight in 1966 when he felt compelled to pen these words to one of the stewardesses. It must have been quite a flight! The letter is poetic, romantic and bold but did it lead to anything or did it capture a mere moment in time, like ships that pass in the night?

Dear Lady,

There is something not quite definable in your face – something lovely, not pretty in a conventionally thought of way. You have something graceful and tender and feminine (sp). You seem to be a woman who has been loved in her childhood, or else, somehow by the mystery of genetic phenomena you have been visited by the gifts of refinement, dignity and poise. Perhaps you cannot be accredited with all that.

Irrespective of your gothic aspects, you have passed something on in terms of your expression, mien and general comportment that is unusual and rewarding.

It's been a pleasant if brief encounter and I wish you well and I hope we shall have occasion to cross eyes again sometime.

Best wishes

Marlon Brando

Apologies

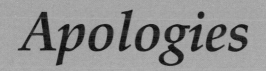

'Never ruin an apology with an excuse'

Benjamin Franklin

PARTNERS

*I'm sorry for the things I said.
I hope you can see that I didn't
mean any of them; they were just
angry words used to hurt you and
I regret every single one. Please
forgive me and give me a chance to
make amends.*

**I said some terrible things, which
I didn't mean. I had let myself
get annoyed by other things and I
took it out on you. I hope you can
forgive me and accept my apology.
I love you and I'm sorry I hurt you.**

*I was wrong. You were right.
I'm sorry.*

Please forgive me for the way I treated you. I took you for granted and ran the risk of losing you for good. I can't believe I was so stupid and cruel and I hope you can see that this was not in my nature.

★ ★

They say that 'sorry' is the hardest word but it's not as hard as 'goodbye'. So I hope you will accept my apology and we can rebuild our relationship before it's too late. You mean the world to me.

★ ★

Can you find it in your heart to forgive me for what I did? I can't claim that I was stupid or confused or any of those excuses. I knew what I was doing and thought I could get away with it. But now it's done, I am struggling to understand why I ever wanted to do it in the first place. It's made me realize that you are everything to me, and I would be lost without you.
I'm so sorry.

PARENTS

Sorry for the way I spoke to you. It was insolent and hurtful and I regret every word. I thought I was being grown-up but I can see now that I was being immature. I have learnt from it and I will handle these situations better in future. Please forgive me.

Dad, I let you down and I'm sorry. I wanted to make you proud of me but I was misguided in the way I went about it. I am so sorry if I caused you embarrassment and I promise it won't happen again. It's been a sobering experience in every sense of the word!

❦

I'm so sorry we haven't been to see you for a while. You are always in my thoughts and in my heart, but life has been hectic lately and I just haven't been able to make plans. I hope you're not hurt by our absence and I promise we will come and see you soon.

I'm so sorry but we won't be able to come on the [date]. It was very kind of you to invite us, but we have another engagment we can't get out of. I'm sorry if this is a disappointment to you, but I hope you understand the situation. Please keep in touch.

I've been doing some thinking and I can see that I was largely to blame for what happened between us. I would like to apologize for the way I behaved and some of the things I said, none of which were meant, I promise. I hope we can move on from this and find a way to settle our differences in a more constructive way. I love you.

★ ★

I'm sorry about the damage that was caused to the house. I should have had more respect for your property and I shouldn't have gone behind your back as I did. I hope you will let me put things right and that I can earn your trust once again.

CHILDREN

I'm sorry I shouted at you. I was frustrated and tired and lost my temper. You were not to blame and I hope you don't feel I meant any of the things I said. I love you and always will.

I'm sorry I got annoyed with you today. I was too wrapped up in my own ambitions and didn't stop to think about the effect it was having on you. I can see now how hurtful that must have been and I hope you will accept my apology. I'm very, very sorry.

I'm sorry I forgot to keep my promise. I know you were relying on me and I let you down. It wasn't through lack of care or love, I simply ran out of time. I wish I could wind back the clock and make everything right but I know I've hurt you and I apologize. Please forgive me.

I'm sorry I missed your big occasion. I would have done anything to get free in time to be there, but it was beyond my power.

I'm sorry I wasn't there for you when you needed me. Throughout your life I have tried to support you whenever you needed me and it pains me that I was absent on this occasion.

I know you have had to endure a lot of pain recently and I am very sorry about that. I want you to know that what has happened between me and dad/mom is in no way down to you. In fact, you are the last bond that ties us and we both want to make this as painless for you as we can. I'm sorry that hasn't been the case, but we will try to make things better for you from now on.

Please forgive me for speaking to you in the way I did. I care so much about you and when things appear to be going wrong I get frustrated, and panic. I didn't mean what I said and I wish I could have found better words to express my concerns. I'm sorry I hurt you and I hope we can start again.

SIBLINGS

I'm sorry we fell out. I said some things I regret and I want you to know that your love for me as a brother/sister means more to me than anything else that might come between us.

I've given a lot of thought to what happened between us and I've decided the only way to make amends is to apologize. We both said some hurtful things and I am sorry for my part in that. I hope you can accept my apology and that we can find some way to repair the bond between us.

—⁓—

I'm sorry it's been so long since I got in touch. It's a sad fact that we tend to neglect the people who are closest to us on the assumption that they will always be there. I promise to make more effort not to be guilty of that again. I love you and miss you and I can't wait to see you again.

OTHER RELATIONS

I'm sorry I missed your birthday. I hope you
will accept my belated best wishes
and a promise to tie a knot in my trunk
for next year!

I'm sorry I was unable to make your party. It
would have been great to see you and all the
family and I was really disappointed that I
couldn't come. I hope it all went well and you
had a great time!

*I'm sorry to hear you and Mom haven't
been getting on lately. If there is something
I can do to help build bridges between
you, please let me know. There is nothing I
would like more than to see the two of you
getting on again like your old selves.*

*I'm sorry you felt unable to attend our
party and I hope it's nothing I've done to
offend you. If it is I apologize and I hope we
can talk about it and sort it out. A family
divided is like a tank that's lost its tracks.*

FRIENDS

I heard that you were upset by something I said last time we were together and I just wanted to apologize for whatever it was. I never intended to hurt you and I am deeply sorry if I did. I hope we can sort this out and move on.

Sorry I haven't been returning your calls lately. I enjoy our chats so much, but I've been having a bit of a difficult time and I just didn't want that to spoil our usual fun. I'm feeling better now and I promise to keep in touch more often.

With deep regret I have to inform you that I won't be able to attend your wedding as I have been double booked. I can't believe the misfortune of this coincidence and I assure you that if there was anything I could do to change it I wouldn't hesitate. Please accept my heartfelt apologies and allow me to make it up to you in some way, to be decided.

I'm sorry if you thought I was being rude when I texted you. You know how these things can come across the wrong way. I want you to know it was supposed to be a joke and I'm sorry it misfired.

I'm so sorry for what I did to you. It was thoughtless and selfish and I wouldn't blame you if you never wanted to spend another second in my company again. I hope that's not the case, though, because I really value your friendship. Please forgive me.

We're sorry for the way we treated you. You were on your own and we took advantage of that to try to get our point across. We can see now that that was wrong and we hope you can forgive us.

I'm sorry we fell out the other day. I don't know what I was thinking about, arguing with my best friend in that way, and I'm deeply embarrassed about some of the things I said. I hope you can forgive me because I love you more than any other friend and would hate to lose you.

NEIGHBOURS

We are having a party tomorrow night and I'd just like to apologize in advance if the noise disturbs you. This is a one-off celebration and we would thank you for your understanding.

★

Apologies for parking across your drive. I only expected to be there for a few seconds, but things got out of hand. I hope it didn't cause you too much inconvenience and I promise it won't happen again.

★ ★

Sorry about the tree in your back garden. We are making arrangements to have it removed as soon as possible and we thank you for your patience. We will make good any damage.

Sorry if you were disturbed by the noise coming from our house last night. I have had a word with the children and they will make more effort to keep it down in future.

'The injured party does not want to be compensated because he has been wronged; he wants to be healed because he has been hurt.'

G K Chesterton

Thank yous

'As we express our gratitude, we must never forget that the highest appreciation is not to utter words, but to live by them.'

John F Kennedy

PRESENTS

You are so kind to have bought me such a fabulous gift. It really does mean a great deal to me and I am touched by your generosity.
Thank you.

—⋙—

I was deeply moved to receive your wonderful gift. I have been spoiled with many lovely presents, but yours was particularly touching and I am so grateful to you for going to such lengths.

Please pass on my thanks to everyone for the beautiful present you bought me. I am touched by their generosity and I would like them to know that I will count this gift among my most treasured possessions.

Thank you very much for the birthday present you gave me. It was just what I wanted and I will get many hours of enjoyment out of it.

You are naughty! I said no presents but I'm glad you disobeyed me! This really is a very lovely thing to have and you are so thoughtful to have bought it for me. Thank you very much.

I am writing to express my gratitude for the generous gift you bought me. It was very kind of you to think of me and to take the trouble to buy me a present. Thank you!

DUTY/HONOR

Thank you so much for asking me to be the godmother/godfather of your child. It would be an honor to fulfil that role and I promise I will take my responsibilities very seriously indeed.

We are writing to thank you for the wonderful job you did at our wedding. We had so many nice comments about you and the role you played in making the whole day such a happy and entertaining occasion for us and all the guests. You will always be a key feature in our memories of the day.

I was bowled over when you asked me to be your best man. There is no shortage of good friends who would have leapt at this chance, so I am deeply honored that you chose me. I look forward to arranging your stag party and helping to make sure your wedding day is really one to remember.

I would like to thank you for choosing me for this special role. It really has made me proud and I will do my best to justify your selection.

Thank you for asking me to speak at your father's funeral. I would be very happy to oblige. There are so many wonderful memories and fond feelings that I would like to express and I feel deeply honored that you have given me this opportunity.

Many thanks for stepping in at the last minute and doing such a professional job. We put you in a very difficult situation but you handled it magnificently. Thank you!

I am writing on behalf of all the family to express our gratitude for the wonderful job you did at my mother's funeral. You were very dear to her and she would have been deeply moved by the warm tribute you paid her. Thanks to you, the occasion was a fitting send-off.
Thank you so much.

PARTIES/EVENTS

Many thanks for inviting us to your party. It sounds like a wonderful occasion and we wouldn't miss it for the world. Please count us in!

Thank you very much for your invitation. We would be delighted to accept and we very much look forward to it.

Thank you for inviting us to your wedding reception. We would love to come. We hope the whole day goes according to plan and that you enjoy every minute.

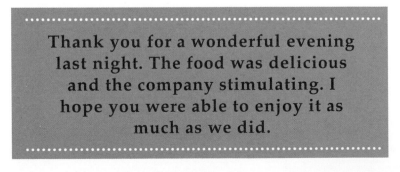

Thank you for a wonderful evening last night. The food was delicious and the company stimulating. I hope you were able to enjoy it as much as we did.

We are writing to thank you for a very enjoyable party. You obviously put in a great deal of time and effort and the result was amazing. We both agreed it's a while since we've been to such a happy and fun occasion and that was entirely down to you.

Thank you for all your efforts in laying on such an entertaining event. Everybody we've spoken to thought it was brilliant and we can't wait for the next one. We hope you enjoyed it as much as we did!

What a superb event you laid on for us! Thank you so much for your generous hospitality. We feel privileged to have been included among your guests and we hope we can reciprocate before too long.

ATTENDANCE

Thank you for joining us in our celebrations. It wouldn't have been the same without you and we were delighted that you could come. We hope you enjoyed it as much as we did!

It was wonderful to see you last night. Thank you very much for coming and helping to make the night go with a bang! We look forward to doing it again very soon.

★

I am writing to express my gratitude to you for attending our event and helping to make it a success. We have received many complimentary comments about your contribution and there is no doubt you were the key to the evening's great success.

HELP/SUPPORT

Just a quick note to say thank you for all your help. I really appreciate you giving up so much of your time and I couldn't have done it without you.

—⁓—

I am really grateful for all the time and effort you put in to helping me with the event last week. You were an invaluable member of the team and it's largely thanks to you that it was all such a success.

I just wanted to write to thank you for all your help recently. I know I have preyed on your time probably more than I should have but you have been so patient and kind and I want you to know that I am extremely grateful. You are one in a million!

Many thanks for all your help and support. We couldn't have done it without you.

Thank you for looking after me through this difficult time. Your support has been a real help for me and I am so grateful for your kindness and generosity. It means the world to me.

Words cannot express how much I value the support you have given me. Many people would have grown tired of my moaning, but you have remained constant throughout, a real rock in my stormy sea. I love you for that and am eternally grateful.

Thank you so much for being there for me. I can't believe how generous you have been with your time and how selfless in always coming when I needed you. I hope I can be that valuable for someone one day.

FRIENDSHIP

Your friendship has kept me going in recent weeks and I want to thank you for all you do for me. Thank you so much.

I am so lucky to have you as a friend. You have been a tremendous support to me lately and I want to thank you for everything you do. Your humor, generosity and positive outlook have helped me through a very difficult time.

You are a wonderful friend and I just want to thank you for that. Your friendship is so effortless, it would be easy to take it for granted, but I want you to know that I am always thankful that you choose to bestow your kindness and affection on me.

Thank you for being you. You are the sweetest, funniest, warmest friend a girl could have and I want you to know that I count my lucky stars every day since I met you.

You have been a terrific ally during my recent troubles and I am so happy to have had you near. You are resolute, loyal and formidable and I would always want you by my side. Thank you!

What an amazing friend you are. You listen when I need to talk, talk when I need to listen and when all else fails, you are there with a hug. Thank you for being so wonderful!

At times like this you find out who your friends really are. You have been an incredible support and without you I would have crumbled to dust. Thank you so much for your loyalty. It means the world to me.

Thank you for making me laugh when I thought the sky was falling in. You are a dear and precious friend.

Thank you for arranging such a wonderful surprise! You must have gone to great lengths to plan that and it meant so much to me that anyone should do that on my behalf. You are a true friend.

Thank you so much for the lovely present. A gift from you is something I always cherish and you have a wonderful way of knowing what I like.

———❦———

Thank you for letting me stay with you while I sorted myself out. The space you gave me was vital in helping me to find my feet again and I will always value the friendship you showed me in my darkest hour.

Thank you for your advice and for listening to my problems. You helped me see the light at the end of the tunnel and gave me the courage to go and find it. That is true friendship.

SYMPATHY

Thank you for taking the trouble to write. Your words of sympathy were much appreciated and helped us to see the positives during this sad time.

We are very grateful for your card and the touching comments you wrote about [name]. It is heartening to know he/she meant so much to so many people and we will always cherish those thoughts.

It was very thoughtful of you to take the trouble to write. I enjoyed reading your recollections of [name] and they helped me to stay cheerful amid my grief. Thank you.

Thank you for your card. I was very touched by your comments and I want you to know that they have been helpful in enabling me to overcome my grief. Your consideration is much appreciated.

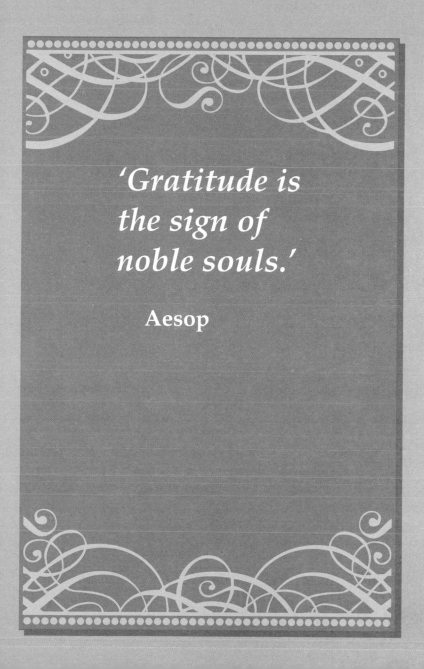

'Gratitude is
the sign of
noble souls.'

Aesop

James Joyce

Irish novelist James Joyce met his muse, Nora Barnacle, a chambermaid, in June 1904. They ran away to Italy together and had two children, Giorgio and Lucia. Their relationship would become strained, although they eventually married in 1931, but in the early months of their affair Joyce was clearly besotted, as this letter reveals.

It has just struck me. I came in at half past eleven. Since then I have been sitting in an easy chair like a fool. I could do nothing. I hear nothing but your voice. I am like a fool hearing you call me 'Dear.' I offended two men today by leaving them coolly. I wanted to hear your voice, not theirs.

When I am with you I leave aside my contemptuous, suspicious nature. I wish I

felt your head on my shoulder. I think I will go to bed.

I have been a half-hour writing this thing. Will you write something to me? I hope you will. How am I to sign myself? I won't sign anything at all, because I don't know what to sign myself.

Keeping in Touch

'Each contact with a human being is so rare, so precious, one should preserve it.'

Anais Nin

POSTCARDS

I saw this picture and thought of you. Just wanted you to know you're never far from my mind and I'd love to catch up with you soon.

Just a quick note to say 'hi' and I'm thinking of you. Hope you and the family are well. Let's make plans to meet up.

I just wanted to write and say that, although we're miles apart, you are always close to my heart. Hope to see you some day soon.

This postcard reminds me that it's been a year since I last got in touch. Where does all the time go? I always think of you when I feel the warmth of the sun. I hope you still think of me.

Too much time has passed since last we met, so I'm writing you this card to let you know I haven't forgotten about you. Far from it. You are in my thoughts every day and I am determined to see you again before another year passes by.

They say it's the thought that counts, so hopefully my thinking about sending you this card will make up for not seeing you for so long. You may be out of sight but you are never out of mind.

Thinking of you always. Seeing you not nearly enough. Let's get together soon.

BRIEF NOTES

I popped round to see you but you were out. I hope all is well and I look forward to seeing you soon.

I saw your car and thought I'd leave a quick note to say hello. I trust all is well with you and the family. Call me on [number] and let's arrange a catch-up.

Just a quick note to say I saw your daughter in the show and thought she was wonderful. You must be very proud. Please pass on my congratulations for an excellent performance. I hope to see you soon.

I drove past you the other day and it reminded me that I haven't seen you for ages. It was great to see you looking so well and it would be good to catch up with all your news sometime. Call me on [number].

'Think where man's glory most begins and ends, and say my glory was I had such friends.'

Aesop

Calendar

'We must use time wisely
and forever realize that
the time is always ripe
to do right.'

Nelson Mandela

Name	Occasion	Date

Name	Occasion	Date

Name	Occasion	Date

Name	Occasion	Date

Name	Occasion	Date

Name	Occasion	Date

Name	Occasion	Date

Name	Occasion	Date

Name	Occasion	Date

Name	Occasion	Date

Name	Occasion	Date

Name	Occasion	Date